HOW YOU CAN HEAR THE VOICE OF GOD TODAY

D1297472

GREGORY DICKOW

How You Can Hear the Voice of God Today
©2003 by Gregory Dickow Ministries.

Unless otherwise noted, all Scripture quotations in this
volume are from the *King James Version* of the Bible.

Printed in the United States of America

For information, please write
Gregory Dickow Ministries,
P.O. Box 7000
Chicago, IL 60680
or visit us online at www.changinglives.org.

TABLE OF CONTENTS

How to Hear the Voice of God

Chapter One

The life of every great man and woman in the Bible was marked by the ability to hear and recognize the voice of God.

Think about this . . . if Noah, Abraham, Moses and others could hear the voice of God under the Old Covenant, then we can expect to hear His voice as clearly under the

New Covenant. In fact, as surprising as it may sound, we should be able to hear His voice even better because we are under a better covenant (Hebrews 8:6).

For example, in Genesis chapter six and seven, God told Noah:

- What He was going to do in the earth.
- What Noah was supposed to do about it.
- How Noah was supposed to do it.

God specifically told Abraham to leave his father's house and receive an inheritance (Genesis 12:1-8). God clearly spoke to Moses when He led His people out of Egypt and gave Moses His commandments (Exodus, chapters 3-20).

As clearly as He spoke to these men, He has promised to speak to us as well. Jesus said in John 10:27, "My sheep hear My voice, and I know them, and they follow me."

God has not stopped talking and revealing Himself to His people. The apostle Peter speaks of how he was an eye witness of Jesus' life, ministry and majesty in 2 Peter 1:16-17. He heard when God said, "This is my beloved Son in whom I am well pleased." God spoke audibly and Peter heard it. In fact, Peter heard the audible voice of God on several occasions.

He writes in 2 Peter 1:18, "And this voice which came from heaven we heard, when we were with Him in the holy mount. *Yet we have a more sure word of prophecy..."* What is this more sure word of prophecy? He tells us in verse 20 that it is the prophecy of scripture.

The Bible you hold in your hand is the primary instrument through which God will speak to you. And if you are born again, you have the Spirit of God on the inside of you to lead you, guide you, and speak to you as well.

Let's look at some practical ways in which you can begin to hear the voice of God.

1. Obey Him in the little things that you already know. Luke 16:10 says, "He that is faithful in that which is least is faithful also in much: and he that is unjust in the least is unjust also in much." God is never going to speak to you about big things if you don't first obey Him in the little things. As we are faithful to carry out the simple commands of scripture such as: forgive, serve, tithe, love–then God's voice will become clearer and clearer in areas of life that are more complicated and harder to figure out.

2. Put yourself in a position to hear God's voice. Habakkuk 2:1 says, "I will stand upon my watch, and set me upon the tower, and will watch to see what He will say unto me..."

How do we do this? By waking up in the morning with the sole objective of hearing God's voice. Isaiah 50:4 says, "He awakens me morning by morning to listen."

Start your day by deciding not to do anything until you have spent time listening to God.

In the midst of life's challenges, confusion, financial problems, even threat of safety, hearing His voice will always deliver you. God will always show you a way out if you begin to sensitize your ears and your heart to hearing His voice. God is always speaking but we must develop the habit of listening and recognizing what He is saying. Remember, you are His sheep, and you hear His voice!

3. Listen consistently (morning by morning). Notice the words "morning by morning" in Isaiah 50:4. Each morning we should pray in the spirit, read encouraging scriptures and listen for the voice of God.

Things happen when you apply the law of consistency to anything. If you will consistently start your day listening to God, you will begin to recognize what He is saying to you all the time.

4. Never listen to a voice that's contrary to the Word (2 Peter 1:19). God will never speak something contrary to the Bible. For example, some people have thought God was telling them they didn't need to join a church. However, Psalm 92:13 and 1 Corinthians 12:18 show us that it is God's will (therefore it is His voice) that we be planted in a church that will help us grow and flourish in God!

5. Expect God to speak to you today. Study Hebrews 3 and 4. These chapters focus on understanding how to hear the voice of God. You can hear the voice of God today, but you must keep a soft heart. I will show you how in the next point.

Hebrews 3:15 says, "Today, if you hear His voice, do not harden your heart." Make a decision to listen with a heart of expectation and obedience—Today!

6. *Keep a soft heart.* The surest way to keep a soft heart is by:

> A. Being willing to do whatever He tells you (before He tells you!)
>
> B. Being thankful for what God has done. A thankful heart is a soft heart.
>
> C. Hold nothing against anyone, for any reason. This includes forgiving yourself. Jesus' blood was shed

for your sins, shortcomings and mistakes! He holds nothing against you! So treat yourself and others the way He treats you. You are forgiven!

THE BENEFITS OF HEARING THE VOICE OF GOD

Chapter Two

God loves you so much that He never wants you to be alone! He will be with you wherever you go and speak to you in every situation in which you will listen with a humble heart. Problems increase in our lives when we don't listen to God. Solutions come when we hear from God. Let's look at some of the benefits of hearing God's voice.

1. Rest. Isaiah 28:12 says, "To whom He said, 'This is the rest wherewith you may cause the weary to rest, and this is the refreshing; but they would not hear (listen).'" Rest speaks of refreshing, and the fulfillment of God's promises. Hebrews 3:7-19 shows us that God's people did not enter into His rest because they did not listen to His voice. Therefore, the more we learn to listen to His voice, (with the intent to obey), the more rest, refreshing and fulfillment we will experience.

2. _Peace._ Psalm 85:8 says, "I will hear what God, the Lord will speak. He will speak peace to His godly ones." God promises peace to those who listen. The Hebrew word for peace, "shalom" means "nothing is missing and nothing is broken." It means to be made whole, to be secure, to have confidence and triumph over our opposition.

3. _Forward Progress._ Look at this amazing and telling scripture in Jeremiah 7:23-24: "But this thing I commanded them, saying, 'Obey My voice, and I will be your God. And you shall be My people. And walk in all the ways I have commanded you, that it may be well unto you.' But they hearkened not, nor inclined their ears, but walked in the counsels and the imaginations of their evil heart; and went backward, not forward." Wow! How much clearer can God be? When we pay attention and listen to His voice, we will go forward, make progress and grow. When we don't listen, we will go backward, lose progress and fail.

For the believer who desires to grow, there is absolutely nothing more important in this life than to hear His voice and follow it!

You may say, "But Pastor, how can I really know if it's God's voice that I'm hearing or if it's just me?"

Well, fortunately, your spirit is made in the image of God, so sometimes, the voice you are hearing is the same voice. Your spirit often "echoes" what God is saying.

Romans 8:16 says, "The Spirit Himself bears witness with our spirit..." In other words, they sound very similar. But to give you some guidelines, you can know it's God's voice when:

    A. It agrees with the scripture.

    B. It agrees with love.

    C. It brings that peace that "surpasses comprehension."

    D. It brings comfort, encouragement and confidence.

    E. It agrees with the character, love and grace of the Lord Jesus Christ.

4.   Supernatural   Deliverance.   In 2 Samuel 5:17-23 David seeks for direction from God on what to do about the Philistine army. God then speaks to him and gives him a strategy that results in David's victory and his enemy's defeat. This is exactly what God will do for you when you listen for His voice. But keep in mind, His strategy will not always make sense to your "natural" mind. You must be "spiritually" minded (Romans 8:5-6).

5. Favor! Proverbs 8:33-35 says, "Hear instruction, and be wise, and refuse it not.

Blessed is the man that heareth me, watching daily at my gates, waiting at the posts of my doors. For whoso findeth me findeth life, and shall obtain favour of the LORD."

As you listen to the voice of God, (which is the highest form of wisdom) God will open doors for you that no man can close. He will surround you with favor as a shield. And, you will experience His provision, protection and promotion!

Again, it is critical to make a decision, in advance, that you will do whatever He tells you to do *before* He tells you. Jesus said in John 7:17, "Do you want to know whether what I said is from God? Be willing to do it first, and then you will know." (Paraphrased translation).

When we do not do what He tells us to do, our heart begins to harden. It's essential that we keep a soft heart as we discussed in the previous chapter. Hebrews 3:7 says "Today, if you hear His voice, do not harden your heart." So, we see here that a soft heart is an obedient heart. Obeying God in the simple things will keep your heart soft. A soft heart can also be defined as: A willingness to listen and a willingness to change.

THE VOICE OF LOVE

Chapter Three

As I stated in the last chapter, one of
the ways to identify and recognize the voice
of God is that His voice always agrees
with love. God is Love. If you are hearing
love, you are usually hearing God. If you
are hearing retaliation, bitterness, unkind
thoughts toward others, and things like these,
you are definitely hearing an ungodly voice.
In fact, if you are hearing things like, "You're

a failure," or "You're not going to make it," or "look at all your mistakes, you can't recover," then this is not the voice of love; therefore it is not the voice of God!

Look at the first thing God spoke to Jesus that we have recorded in the Bible. After Jesus came up out of the waters of baptism, Mark 1:11 records the voice of God–the voice of love: "And there came a voice from heaven, saying 'You are My beloved Son, in whom I am well pleased.'"

Notice before Jesus ever ministered, before He ever performed a miracle, God spoke to Him about His love for Him. God's love was not based on Jesus' performance. His love was completely unconditional. He called Him, "My beloved."

This was the most important and foundational Word from God that Jesus received. And it is the most important thing we can ever hear from God. "I love you. You're Mine."

If we fail to hear the voice of love, we will fail to hear the voice of God. There were many other things that God spoke to Jesus and there will be many other things that He will speak to you, but none as important as "I love you." Furthermore, it will be incredibly difficult for you to hear anything else from God, if you don't first hear "love."

When God says "I love you," He means three things:

1. I will never leave you (Hebrews 13:5).

2. I will never break my promises to you (Deuteronomy 7:8-9, Judges 2:1).

3. I will never remember your sins anymore. (Hebrews 8:12).

Upon this holy foundation of the voice of God's love, we can begin to accurately hear His voice. Many people have a distorted view of God's love and therefore cannot hear His voice.

I strongly encourage you to meditate on the verses I have listed above and embrace this concept: that hearing the voice of God begins with hearing the voice of love. This revelation will open the door to everything else God wants to speak to you and everything else God wants to do in your life!

HINDRANCES TO HEARING THE VOICE OF GOD

Chapter Four

Now that we see how powerful God's voice can be in our lives, let's remove some of the hindrances that are keeping us from hearing His voice.

1. Hardness of heart. As we mentioned earlier, when you don't listen to God's voice, you begin to harden your heart. By hardening your heart, you make it even more difficult to hear what God is trying to say. It will also make it more difficult for you to believe what He has already said. Jesus rebuked His disciples in Mark 16:14 for unbelief and hardness of heart.

"Afterward He appeared unto the eleven as they sat at meat, and upbraided them for their unbelief and hardness of heart, because they believed not them which had seen him after he was risen."

Unbelief and hardness of heart go hand in hand and must be stopped from gaining further access to your life. So repent! Ask God to forgive you for hardening your heart. Forgive those who have hurt you. Choose to believe what God has said in His Word, whether it makes sense to you or not; whether you "feel it" or not. Then go back to the simple things that you may have allowed to slip.

Go back to the last thing you know God told you to do and do it. Go back to obeying Him in the little things, and His voice will become clearer and clearer. You will put yourself in position to receive the supernatural benefits of hearing from Him.

2. *Limiting God and yourself.* Mark 9:23 says, "All things are possible to him who believes." You need to believe whatever God says. Jesus is saying "Go ahead and believe—All things will be possible to you." Don't limit God! Don't limit yourself!

Ephesians 3:20 says, "Now unto him that is able to do exceeding abundantly above all that we ask or think, according to the power that worketh in us. . . . " He can do exceeding abundantly beyond all you can ask or think. For example, if you think you could never pray for someone and see them get healed, you're limiting God. These signs will follow those who believe . . . (Mark 16:17-18). In Philippians 4:13, God promises that you can do all things through Christ, which is in you and will strengthen you. Take the limits off of what you think God could say to you or ask you to do. And when you do, you will take the limits off of yourself as well.

3. Unfinished Business. Some people want to hear from God, but they haven't done what God has already asked them to do. Historians believe it took Noah up to 100 years to build the ark. And what is interesting is, we don't see any record of God saying anything else to him from the time he started to the time he finished (Genesis 6:13; Genesis 7:1). So, finish the last thing you know God has shown you to do and then expect Him to tell you what to do next.

What do you do when it seems as if God is silent? The last thing He told you to do.

4. *Not being faithful in money.* Luke 16:10 says, "He who is faithful in what is least (money) is also faithful in much." If God can't trust you with "unimportant" things (such as money), how can He trust you with the true riches. Material things are our training ground. We must show Him we can be faithful with material things and then He will trust us with spiritual and supernatural things. So the "unimportant things" are important things because they demonstrate our faithfulness to God!

When you remove these hindrances, and begin to take some of the practical steps to listen with a heart of expectation and obedience, you will begin to experience the benefits of hearing the voice of God. Begin today! You will never be the same again!

About the Author

Gregory Dickow is the host of "Changing Your Life," a dynamic television show seen throughout the world, reaching a potential 450 million households. He is also the founder and Senior Pastor of Life Changers International Church, a diverse and thriving congregation in the Chicago area with several thousand in weekly attendance.

Known for his ability to communicate the power and principles of God's Word clearly and concisely, Pastor Dickow lives to see the lives of people dramatically changed forever.

Pastor Dickow is also founder of Valeo International, a family of churches and ministries committed to spreading the Gospel of Jesus Christ, planting churches, and making disciples around the world.